HAND to EARTH

TIME FOR KIDS

Saving the Environment

Jessica Cohn

Consultants

Timothy Rasinski, Ph.D.
Kent State University

Lori Oczkus
Literacy Consultant

Donald L. Coan, Ph.D.

Based on writing from
TIME For Kids. *TIME For Kids* and the *TIME For Kids* logo are registered trademarks of TIME Inc. Used under license.

Publishing Credits

Dona Herweck Rice, *Editor-in-Chief*
Lee Aucoin, *Creative Director*
Jamey Acosta, *Senior Editor*
Lexa Hoang, *Designer*
Stephanie Reid, *Photo Editor*
Rane Anderson, *Contributing Author*
Rachelle Cracchiolo, *M.S.Ed., Publisher*

Image Credits: pp.34, 37 (bottom) iStockphoto; pp.8–9 NASA; p.23 (bottom) AFP/Getty Images/Newscom; p.5 (top) Danita Delimont/Newscom; p.38 (right) Richard Hutchings/Photo Researchers, Inc.; p.29 Timothy J. Bradley/Robin Erickson; pp.6–7, 15–16 Timothy J. Bradley; All other images from Shutterstock.

Teacher Created Materials
5301 Oceanus Drive
Huntington Beach, CA 92649-1030
http://www.tcmpub.com
ISBN 978-1-4333-4868-6

Table of Contents

Extreme Effects

Extreme weather is everywhere. Heavy rains are pouring down on India. Wildfires are breaking out across California's dry mountains. Deserts are getting larger. At the same time, arctic ice is shrinking. **Glaciers** (GLEY-shers) in the north are melting at a faster rate. This means less space for the animals that live there. These animals must move to new areas or die. These are just some examples of the effects of **climate** change on Earth.

Scientists have been studying the changes on Earth for many years. And now they are seeing a pattern. It's unlikely anyone felt the change. But Earth's temperature has increased over the past century. It's about 1.4°F hotter. That doesn't seem like much, but the effects are clear.

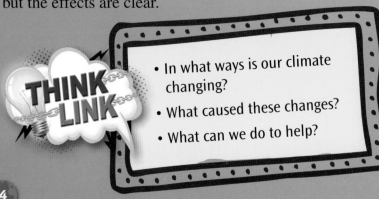

THINK LINK

- In what ways is our climate changing?
- What caused these changes?
- What can we do to help?

Getting Warmer

Many things can raise Earth's temperature. Volcanoes can heat the air. Warm water can raise the temperature of the land. Sunshine can make the air hotter, too. But nearly all scientists agree the main reason for the increase is **greenhouse gases**. These are gases in Earth's atmosphere. They trap the sun's heat. This raises the temperature of the atmosphere. And even small changes in temperature and weather can cause big changes in Earth's climate.

Natural Greenhouse Effect

Greenhouse Gases

Solar Radiation

Reradiated Heat

The Greenhouse Effect

Greenhouse gases include **carbon dioxide**, **methane**, and **water vapor**. These gases occur naturally and keep our planet warm. However, human activities have made more of these gases. These gases have trapped the heat and created a giant greenhouse effect on Earth.

What's the Difference?

Weather is an event that occurs over the course of hours or days. Climate is the average weather conditions in a region over many years.

Cause and Effect

The following human activities contribute to an increase in greenhouse gases:

- Burning fossil fuels
- Deforestation
- Raising livestock
- Factory farming
- Changes in how land is used

Human-Enhanced Greenhouse Effect

More Greenhouse Gases

Reradiated Heat

Solar Radiation

Reradiated Heat

Off the Charts

Scientists collect and analyze **data**. They look at data from the past to make guesses about the future. **Climate models** help scientists look at how conditions on Earth affect other conditions. They use satellites and computers to measure changes. Scientists compare the models with tests they complete in the field. All data shows that the rise of greenhouse gases is making Earth heat up. Scientists are working to find out what is making more of these gases.

Eyes in the Sky

National Aeronautics and Space Administration (NASA) satellites collect data every day. They record information about the atmosphere, the oceans, and the land. They even help **meteorologists** predict the weather. A program called Landsat takes photos of Earth from space. Scientists study the photos to find out what areas need help.

One of NASA's Landsat satellites

This image shows the Lambert Glacier in Antarctica from above. Changes in the ice mean the rest of Earth will experience changes on land and in the air.

Key:
The colors show how fast the ice is moving.

3,200–4,000 feet per year

no motion

320–1,000 feet per year

Human Influence

Scientists are learning there are many reasons for climate change. Using resources is one of them. We all depend on Earth. Its resources let us survive. There are two types of resources. **Renewable resources** can be replaced. They are made again and again in nature. Air, sunlight, and water are all renewable resources. **Nonrenewable resources** are used faster than they can be made. **Fossil fuels** such as coal, gas, and oil are nonrenewable resources.

Both types of resources are important to life on Earth. We need air to breathe. We need sunlight to grow crops. And our bodies need water. Fossil fuels are used to power our homes, schools, and vehicles.

Air, water, and land are all affected. And one change can lead to another change. That means even simple changes may have complex effects.

Ancient Energy

Fossil fuels come from dead plants and animals that are over 300 million years old. They are found underground. It will take millions of years before more fossil fuels will be created.

Fascinating Fuels

Coal looks like a hard black rock. Coal was first used in China 3,000 years ago.

Oil has been used for over 5,000 years. It can be made by turning coal into a liquid. Oil can also be found deep in the ground. It is used to fuel many different vehicles.

Natural gas has been used for over 7,000 years. It burns very easily. The names are similar, but natural gas is different from gasoline. Many homes and businesses use natural gas for heat.

Power Hungry

We use electricity to power our cities and homes. The **generators** that make electricity need heat to run. Most generators burn coal or gas to get the heat. But the effects can be harmful to our environment. In some power plants, water or wind are used to create heat. Some power plants collect the sun's heat. Others use heat from inside the Earth. And there are some that split **atoms**. This type of power makes dangerous waste. Each system has problems.

Most of our energy comes from nonrenewable resources. People are working hard to find new ways to create energy. For example, some new cars run on electricity. This is cleaner than burning gasoline. Yet the electricity is not always made in a clean way. Scientists are looking for better power systems. Meanwhile, using less gas and electricity can help the problem.

About 83 percent of the world's air pollution comes from making and using electricity.

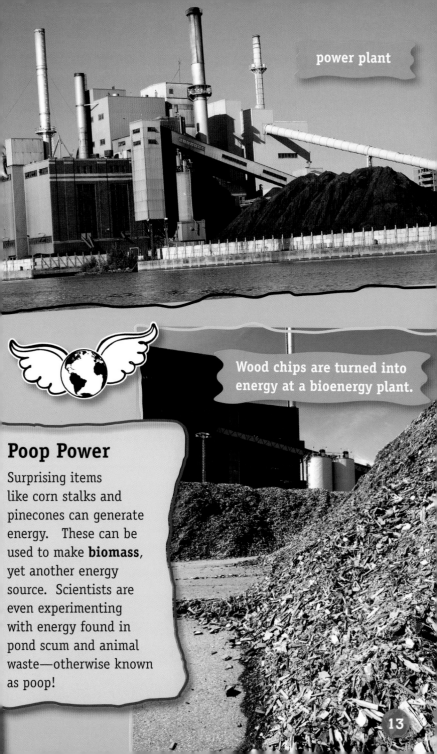

Wood chips are turned into energy at a bioenergy plant.

Poop Power

Surprising items like corn stalks and pinecones can generate energy. These can be used to make **biomass**, yet another energy source. Scientists are even experimenting with energy found in pond scum and animal waste—otherwise known as poop!

Water World

Water is important to all living things. Without it, plants, animals, and people would die. Seventy percent of Earth's surface is covered in water. It may sound like a lot, but only 3 percent is **drinkable**. This water comes from glaciers, ice caps, and groundwater. Water is considered a renewable resource. But it could quickly turn into a nonrenewable resource. If glaciers and ice caps melted into the ocean, there would be nothing left for us to drink! There would be no freshwater for plants, animals, or people.

the edge of a glacier

Wasted Water

In the United States, the average person uses between 80 and 100 gallons of water per day. Long showers, car washes, and large lawns all require water.

Purifying Water

Researchers are studying ways to keep water clean. Water lilies may be a natural way to purify water. The long roots and thick leaves are able to absorb toxic chemicals in water, leaving behind only clean water.

Water Watch

Water is a renewable resource. It has been around for millions of years. How is this possible? The water cycle moves water on, above, and below Earth's surface. It is possible that you have gulped down a glass of water from the same source dinosaurs once drank from!

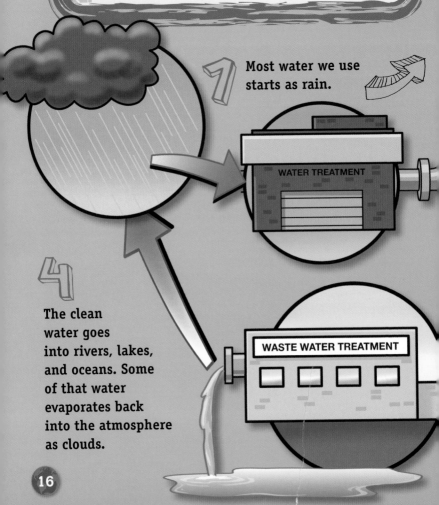

Most water we use starts as rain.

WATER TREATMENT

The clean water goes into rivers, lakes, and oceans. Some of that water evaporates back into the atmosphere as clouds.

WASTE WATER TREATMENT

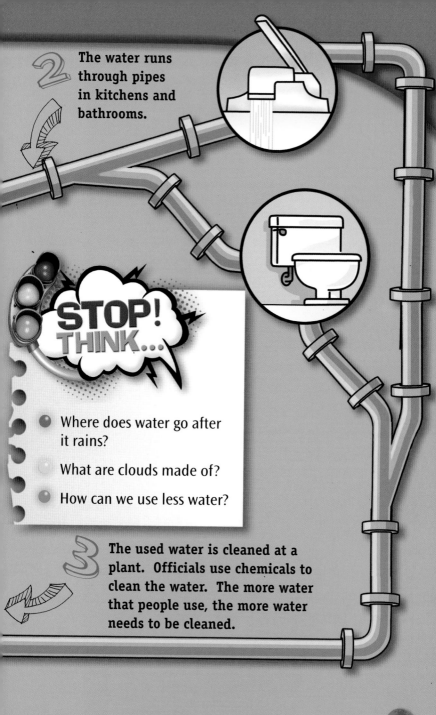

2 The water runs through pipes in kitchens and bathrooms.

STOP! THINK...

- Where does water go after it rains?

- What are clouds made of?

- How can we use less water?

3 The used water is cleaned at a plant. Officials use chemicals to clean the water. The more water that people use, the more water needs to be cleaned.

Food Facts

Plants need food, water, sunlight, and space to grow. To make sure the crops stay healthy, farmers must protect them. Most do this by using **pesticides** and **fertilizers**. The chemicals in these products may create greenhouse gases.

Many resources are used to grow food. Even more resources are needed to **transport** the food to the market. Food is driven from farms and factories around the country. Some of it comes from other countries. It takes a lot of energy to get the food to the grocery store. That energy is used by cars, trucks, planes, trains, and ships that transport goods. But what if food didn't need to travel so far? What if it came from nearby farms or your garden at home? Think of all the energy we could save. Using less energy means making less pollution.

Fast Food

A farmers market is a place where you can buy locally grown food. That food doesn't come from faraway places. It comes from a local farm closer to your house. It doesn't take as much energy to get to you.

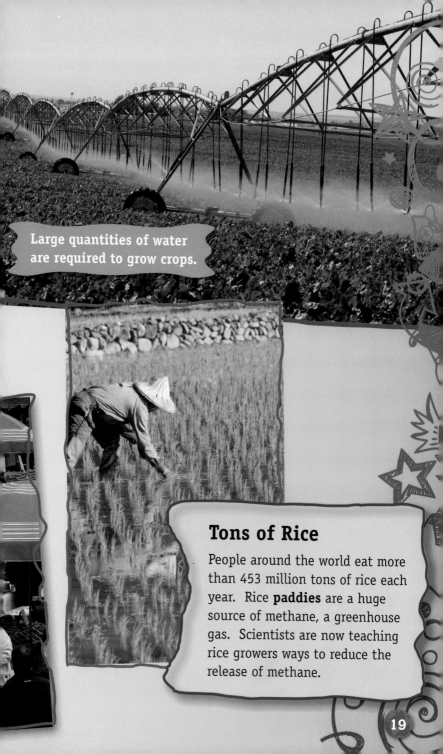

Large quantities of water are required to grow crops.

Tons of Rice

People around the world eat more than 453 million tons of rice each year. Rice **paddies** are a huge source of methane, a greenhouse gas. Scientists are now teaching rice growers ways to reduce the release of methane.

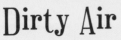
Dirty Air

Smog is a thick haze in the air. It is caused when sunlight strikes on smoke and car **exhaust**. Air is **polluted** in different ways. Cars and factories burn fuel. That fuel sends harmful greenhouse gases into the atmosphere. Natural events, such as volcanic eruptions and wildfires, can also pollute the air. Some pollutants can cause illnesses. Others can make it hard to breathe. They also increase greenhouse gas levels, making the Earth hotter.

Ride a Bike

Smog happens when greenhouse gases build up. It is made up of strong chemicals that harm plants, animals, and people. In some large cities, as much as 85 percent of pollution comes from cars, trucks, and other vehicles. Riding bicycles to school or work lowers pollution rates significantly.

The World Health Organization estimates that 4.6 million people die each year from pollution-related illness.

Losing Ground

Living things need space to survive. As the human **population** increases, we need to build new places to live. But our need for space means taking it from other creatures. **Deforestation** is the process of clearing away areas of forest. About 70 percent of land animals live in forests. When a forest is cut down, animals lose their homes. They must find other places to live and move into new **ecosystems**. When that happens, the new ecosystems change, too.

Deforestation also causes changes in the global climate. Without trees to cover the ground, soil dries out. Most plants don't grow as well in dry soil. This means there is less food for animals. Plants also help decrease greenhouse gases because they consume carbon dioxide. If there are fewer trees, more carbon dioxide stays in the air.

Human homes take away natural space in the environment.

solar energy

oxygen

carbon dioxide

Every tree eliminates one ton of carbon dioxide from the atmosphere in its lifetime.

Nearly half of the Amazon Rainforest may be lost by the year 2050.

Every second, a piece of a rainforest the size of a football field is cut down.

Twists and Turns

DIG DEEPER!

The only thing worse than dry soil is no soil at all. Much of the Earth is being covered with hard materials such as pavement and cement. As cities grow, there is less room for plants to grow. One of the ways to help the environment is to stop paving over so much of our world. Check out some of the longest roads in the world.

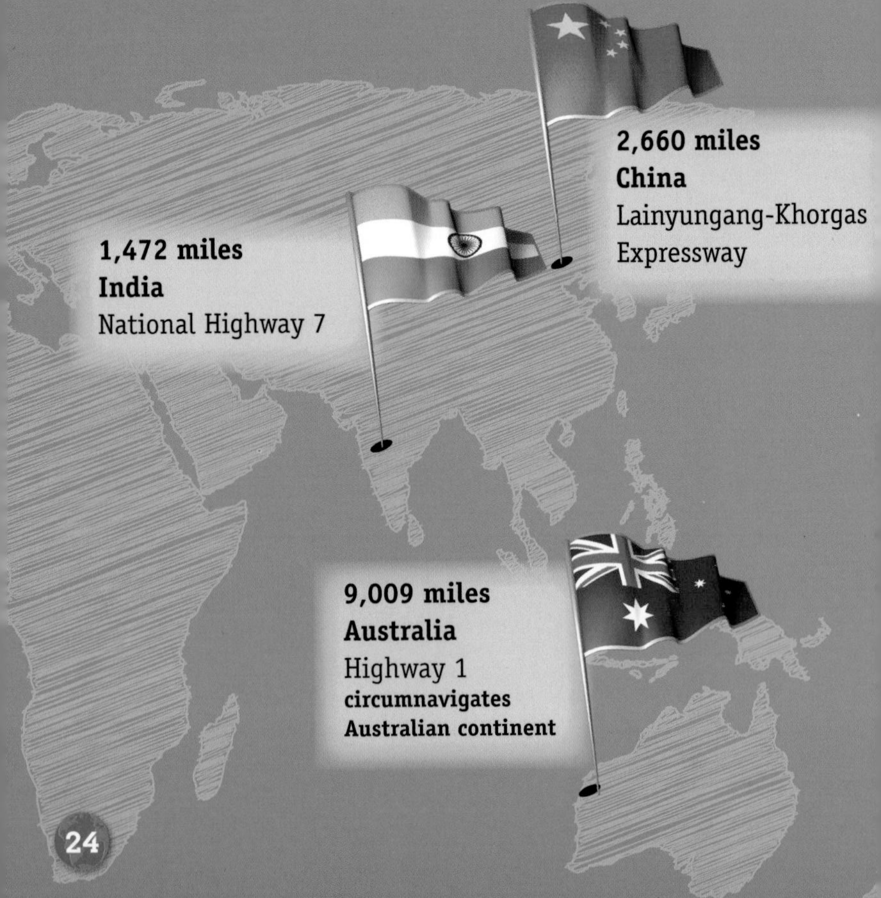

2,660 miles
China
Lainyungang-Khorgas Expressway

1,472 miles
India
National Highway 7

9,009 miles
Australia
Highway 1
circumnavigates
Australian continent

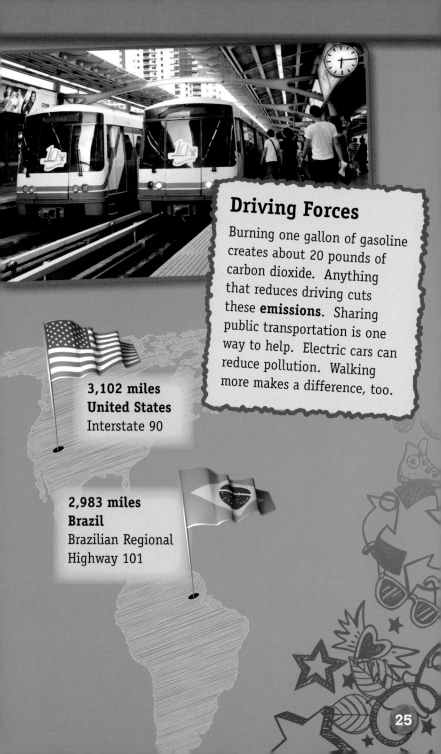

Driving Forces

Burning one gallon of gasoline creates about 20 pounds of carbon dioxide. Anything that reduces driving cuts these **emissions**. Sharing public transportation is one way to help. Electric cars can reduce pollution. Walking more makes a difference, too.

3,102 miles
United States
Interstate 90

2,983 miles
Brazil
Brazilian Regional Highway 101

More Means More

Today, there are almost seven billion people on Earth. But just 2,000 years ago, there were only 250 million people. Each year, 130 million babies are born. People are living longer. The population is increasing. The more people we have on Earth, the more resources that will be used up. We must be smarter about using resources. With so many people, every bit helps.

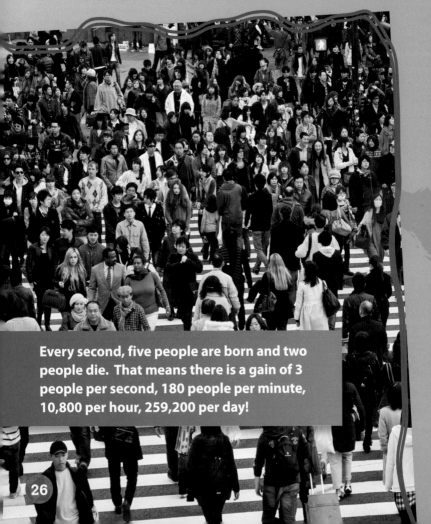

Every second, five people are born and two people die. That means there is a gain of 3 people per second, 180 people per minute, 10,800 per hour, 259,200 per day!

Human Numbers through Time

The population has been growing rapidly. And more people are expected in the future!

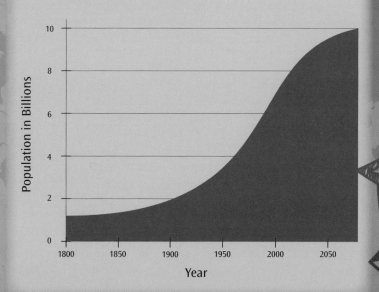

Trash Talk

All those people make a lot of trash! Each American makes about 4.6 pounds of trash each day. **Recycling** even one glass bottle can help. It saves some of the energy needed to make another one. That same amount of energy could power a lightbulb for four hours. Americans use one billion shopping bags every year. That adds up to 300,000 tons of waste! And that's 300,000 tons of waste that could be avoided. Taking cloth bags to the store is an easy way to prevent waste.

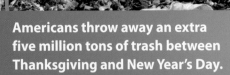

Americans throw away an extra five million tons of trash between Thanksgiving and New Year's Day.

Anatomy of a Trash Can

We create a lot of trash. But most of it can be recycled. Take a look at what we are throwing away.

Other 3.4%

Glass 4.6%

Wood 6.4%

Rubber, Leather, Textiles 8.4%

Metals 9.0%

Plastics 12.4%

Yard Trimmings 13.4%

Food Scraps 13.9%

Paper 28.5%

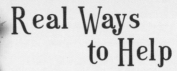

Real Ways to Help

There are lots of ways to help the planet. We can all work together to use fewer resources. Remember these five Rs, and you'll be well on your way.

Reduce

We can cut down on the amount of water used in a shower or while brushing teeth. We can reduce gas by traveling by bike or carpooling.

Reuse

We can reuse cloth napkins. We can wash cups rather than using paper ones.

Did you know appliances use energy even when they are turned off? This is called **phantom power**. Unplug your computer and other machines to reduce energy use.

Recycle

Plastic, paper, and metal can all be recycled.

Over 7,000 communities have pay-as-you-throw programs. Citizens in these cities pay for each bag of trash they throw away. This cuts down on the amount of waste produced because most people don't want to pay a lot of money to dispose of their trash.

Repair

Try fixing things rather than throwing them away.

GARAGE SALE

Rethink

Before buying something new, ask if a used item would work just as well.

31

In Our Hands

Cars, planes, and trains make our lives easier. Electricity lets us work longer and play into the night. But the advantages of modern life have changed our world in important ways. Resources are being used faster than they can be replaced. Less land is available for many forms of life, including humans. Earth is warming up.

But we can solve these problems. And it's our responsibility. Earth needs our help.

"When the well's dry, we know the worth of water."
—Benjamin Franklin

Find Your Footprint

We each leave a mark on the earth. But are the effects good or bad? Every year, we add to the carbon levels in the atmosphere. A **carbon footprint** is a measure of our activities. It shows the amount of fossil fuels that we burn. For example, heating a cup of water uses less fuel than heating a full pot. So the footprint is smaller. Footprints show the pollution made by the products we use.

Families can figure out their footprints online. They can find ways to use less energy. And they can find ways to make less pollution. With your family, make a list of the activities you do every day. Which of those activities use energy? Now, how can you use less energy? Make a plan and stick to it. Work with your family to reduce your carbon footprint.

Go to myfootprint.org to see where you stand.

REDUCE YOUR CARBON FOOT PRINT

Playing board games uses less energy than electronic games.

Tire Tracks

Driving 1,200 miles per month releases 0.5 tons of carbon dioxide into the atmosphere. That is six tons of carbon dioxide per year, per person. What can you do to leave a better mark on Earth?

Follow Your Passion

Many groups are raising awareness about environmental issues. Think about what you like to do and what you're good at. These are the best ways you can help the planet. Do you like talking to people? Let others know about ways they can help the environment. Do people tell you that you should be a writer? Then start a blog about ways to reduce your carbon footprint. Include tips on how your readers can do the same. If you're crafty, try making something new out of something old. What can you make out of that old sweater? If you love being outside, try walking or riding a bike to school instead of driving. As individuals, we lead by example. Together, we can create a better world.

Greener Pastures

Where is your favorite place to spend a lazy Sunday? Whether it's a park, your bedroom, or the mall, every place can use a little help being green. Look for ways to help the environment wherever you are.

At a shop...

look for products with less packaging.

At home...

keep energy costs low by turning off unused lights.

At the park...

ask about planting a tree to add more oxygen to the air.

Protecting Our Planet

As the world changes, we must change, too. The earth is in trouble. And we can't wait to take action. We have the tools to create a healthier planet. But it will take hard work and millions of people to make a difference. Little changes from everyone will make big changes in the world. What can you do today?

WE
RECYCLE

"Each and every one of us can make changes in the way we live our lives and become part of the solution."
— Al Gore

A Group Effort

Kids Korps USA offers ways for young people to help others. Today, many of their efforts are aimed at helping the planet. Robin Chappelow is one of their directors.

Jessica: Which Earth-friendly projects do the kids like best?

Robin: Favorites are **lagoon**, beach, and canyon cleanups. The kids like picking up trash and then tallying what they found for environmental studies.

Jessica: What are other ways kids can help?

Robin: A creative project kids have enjoyed is making seed balls from mud. The balls were filled with coastal sage seeds. We **collaborated** with the Wildlife Research Institute. They spread thousands of these seed balls in places where the plants had burned in wildfires. This was a great way to help grow back the native plants.

Seed Balls

Making seed balls is a fun way to fight deforestation. More plants mean less carbon dioxide in the atmosphere. Follow these simple steps to make our planet cleaner—and more beautiful!

  Mix the seeds, compost, and dry clay.

Ingredients

5 cups of red clay

1 cup of wildflower seeds

3 cups of compost

Water

(Makes 120 seed balls)

Slowly add water. Use just enough water to make a ball the size of a large marble. Balls should be firm.

 Let the seed balls dry.

  Plant the seed balls in a garden, park, or open field.

Glossary

atoms—tiny particles that make up matter

biomass—material made of plant and animal waste

carbon dioxide—a greenhouse gas

carbon footprint—the amount of greenhouse gases created by something during a given time period

climate—the average weather in a region over many years

climate models—representations of the data computers collect about Earth's climate

collaborated—worked together

data—a collection of factual information

deforestation—the action or process of clearing forests

drinkable—water that is safe to drink

ecosystems—areas where certain living and nonliving things relate to one another

emissions—substances given off through energy use, usually in the air

exhaust—used gas or vapor from an engine

fertilizers—solid waste from farm animals that is added to soil to help plants grow

fossil fuels—the fuels made from plant and animal remains

generators—machines that can change energy into electricity

glaciers—large bodies of ice that slowly move down mountains and valleys

greenhouse gases—gases that trap heat in the atmosphere, including carbon dioxide, methane, and water vapor

lagoon—a shallow body of water, usually made by people

meteorologists—people who study weather and Earth's atmosphere

methane—a greenhouse gas

nonrenewable resources—resources that are created by the earth and can't be replaced

paddies—the wet land in which rice is grown

pesticides—chemicals used to kill insects that hurt crops

phantom power—energy used by appliances that are turned off

polluted—spoiled with waste

population—the number of people living in a country or region

recycling—processing materials such as glass, metal, or paper for reuse

renewable resources—resources that are created and replaced by the Earth

smog—a thick haze caused by sunlight striking on smoke and exhaust

transport—to move from one place to another

water vapor—water that is suspended in air as a gas

Index

Bibliography

Amsel, Sheri. *The Everything Kids' Environment Book.* **Adams Media, 2007.**

Through simple activities, this book shows things you can do to help protect the planet every day.

Caduto, Michael J. *Catch the Wind, Harness the Sun.* **Storey Publishing, 2011.**

This book has 22 activities and experiments focused on producing and playing with renewable energy.

David, Laurie and Cambria Gordon. *The Down-to-Earth Guide To Global Warming.* **Orchard Books, 2007.**

This book is filled with facts about global warming and its consequences. It also includes suggestions on how you can help combat global warming in your home, school, and community.

Housel, Debra J. *Pioneering Ecologists.* **Teacher Created Materials, 2008.**

Meet the scientists who study the connections that living things have with one another and their surroundings.

Javna, Sophie. *The New 50 Simple Things Kids Can Do to Save the Earth.* **Andrews McMeel Publishing, 2009.**

This book gives more information on how to find your carbon footprint and how to make a difference with simple projects, tips, and little-known facts.

More to Explore

Container Recycling Institute
http://www.container-recycling.org/kids.htm

This website describes different recycling programs that other kids have started at their schools.

Environmental Protection Agency
http://www.epa.gov/peya

This program promotes awareness of America's natural resources and recognizes youth across the country for protecting our nation's air, water, land, and ecology.

World Water Monitoring Challenge
http://www.worldwatermonitoringday.org

World Water Monitoring Challenge is an international education program that involves the public in protecting water resources around the world. You can monitor and register the quality of local water bodies by using a simple test kit. The results are then submitted to the website and included in the annual report.

Crafts Made from Recyclables
http://familyfun.go.com/crafts/crafts-by-material/recyclable-projects

Take household items and turn them into something fun and new. This website has lots of ideas for creative recyclable crafts.

Kids for Saving Earth
http://www.kidsforsavingearth.org

Kids for Saving Earth has all kinds of information on how to protect the land, air, water, and creatures. Learn ways to protect Earth and make smart Earth-friendly choices.

About the Author

Jessica Cohn grew up in Michigan, where she volunteered for conservation projects in school and the Girl Scouts. She has a bachelor's degree in English and a master's in written communications. She has worked in educational publishing for more than a decade as a writer and an editor. She has written articles and books on many subjects, including the health of our planet. She is married and has two sons. Growing up around the Great Lakes made her especially aware of the importance of clean water.